# 150+
# Ridiculously Funny
# YO MAMA
# JOKES

© Copyright by Bim Bam Bom Funny Joke Books. Images Feepik.com or licensed for commercial use. All rights reserved.

## Table of Contents

3. YO MOMMA is SO DUMB
11. YO MOMMA is SO FAT
19. YO MOMMA is SO UGLY
23. YO MOMMA is SO STUPID
27. YO MOMMA is SO OLD
31. YO MOMMA is SO HAIRY
33. YO MOMMA is SO SHORT
35. YO MOMMA is SO BALD
36. YO MOMMA is SO NASTY
37. YO MOMMA is SO MUCH ELSE!

# YO MOMMA IS SO DUMB...

Yo momma is so dumb...she tripped over a cordless phone!

Yo momma is so dumb...she asked for a price check at the Dollar Store!

Yo momma is so dumb...when she went to the World Cup she brought tea bags!

Yo momma is so dumb...when I told her it was chilly outside, she went to the kitchen to get a plate!

# YO MOMMA IS SO DUMB...

Yo momma is so dumb...she once opened a bag of M&M's and tried to put them in alphabetical order!

Yo momma is so dumb...it takes her an hour and a half to make minute rice!

Yo momma is so dumb...she went back to Dunkin' Donuts to return a donut because it had a hole in it!

Yo momma is so dumb...she tried to surf the microwave!

# YO MOMMA IS SO DUMB...

Yo momma is so dumb...where it said, "Do not write here" on her application, she wrote "Ok"!

Yo momma is so dumb...she got stabbed at a shoot out!

Yo momma is so dumb...she doesn't know which date 9/11 is on!

Yo momma is so dumb...she returned a puzzle to the store because she thought it was broken!

# YO MOMMA IS SO DUMB...

Yo momma is so dumb...when thieves broke into her house and stole the coffee machine, she followed them outside and yelled to them, "Hey, you forgot the coffee!"

Yo momma is so dumb...when someone asked her what the capital of Canada was she answered, "C!"

Yo momma is so dumb...when her phone broke down she called Taco Bell!

Yo momma is so dumb...I once saw her trying to drown a fish!

# YO MOMMA IS SO DUMB...

Yo momma is so dumb...I saw her put two quarters in her ears and then she thought she was listening to a 50 Cent record!

Yo momma is so dumb...she watches "The Three Stooges" and takes notes!

Yo momma is so dumb...she climbed over a glass wall to see what was on the other side!

Yo momma is so dumb...she came to a stop sign and waited till it said go!

# YO MOMMA is SO DUMB...

Yo momma is so dumb...she got hit by a parked car.

Yo momma is so dumb...her password needed 8 characters, so she typed "Snow White and the 7 dwarfs."

Yo momma is so dumb...she thought Bruno Mars was a planet.

Yo momma is so dumb...when she was hungry she went to the Apple Store to get an apple.

Yo momma is so dumb...she told me sharks smoke seaweed.

# YO MOMMA IS SO DUMB...

Yo momma is so dumb...when she came over to my house but didn't find me at home, she left me a voicemail by shouting in my mailbox!

Yo momma is so dumb...she thought she could freeze time by putting her watch in the fridge!

Yo momma is so dumb...when she watched the CBS show '60 Minutes', it took her 2 hours!

Yo momma is so dumb...she took a ruler to bed to see how long she slept!

# YO MOMMA IS SO DUMB...

Yo momma is so dumb...she tried to make an appointment with Dr. Pepper!

Yo momma is so dumb...she put the air conditioning in backwards saying she was going to chill outside!

Yo momma is so dumb...when your family was driving in the car to Disneyland, she noticed a sign that said "Disneyland left," so she turned around to go home.

Yo momma is so dumb...she once tried to climb Mountain Dew.

# YO MOMMA IS SO FAT...

Yo momma is so fat...when she went on the scale it said, "To be continued..."

Yo momma is so fat...when the photographer pointed the camera at her and said "Cheese", she asked, "Where?"

Yo momma is so fat...her shadow broke the sidewalk in two!

Yo momma is so fat...when she applied to be a bus driver, they told her she was qualified to be the bus!

# YO MOMMA IS SO FAT...

Yo momma is so fat...when she did a push-up, planet Earth went down!

Yo momma is so fat...she put on a Malcolm X T-shirt, and a helicopter tried to land on her!

Yo momma is so fat...she couldn't get in or out when she went to get a burger at In and Out!

Yo momma is so fat...her Patronus is a cake!

Yo momma is so fat...she wears an asteroid belt!

# YO MOMMA IS SO FAT...

Yo momma is so fat...she is the circle of life that Elton John sang about in The Lion King!

Yo momma is so fat...and old, when Moses wanted to part the Red Sea, he told her to do a cannon ball!

Yo momma is so fat...when she walked in front of the television, I missed three commercials!

Yo momma is so fat...when she went for a swim, Columbus claimed her for new land!

# YO MOMMA IS SO FAT...

Yo momma is so fat...Earth tilted when she fell off the couch!

Yo momma is so fat...she got stuck when she jumped for joy!

Yo momma is so fat...she got baptized at Sea World!

Yo momma is so fat...when she went to the zoo, the hippos got jealous!

Yo momma is so fat...she has her own area code!

# YO MOMMA IS SO FAT...

Yo momma is so fat...when she went to KFC the cashier asked, "What size bucket?" and yo momma said, "The one on the roof"!

Yo momma is so fat...she sat on the rainbow and Skittles came out!

Yo momma is so fat, one day she sat on an iPod and made the iPad!

Yo momma is so fat...when she fell in love she broke it!

# YO MOMMA IS SO FAT...

Yo momma is so fat...she causes a tsunami when she sweats.

Yo momma is so fat...she wakes up on both sides of the bed in the morning.

Yo momma is so fat...when she turned on her PS4 the PlayStation Network crashed.

Yo momma is so fat...her butt has its own congressman!

Yo momma is so fat...when she auditioned for Star Wars she was cast as outer space!

# YO MOMMA IS SO FAT...

Yo momma is so fat...she needs cheat codes for Wii Fit!

Yo momma is so fat...her stomach has a cell phone, to call her mouth when it's time to eat!

Yo momma is so fat...when she went whale watching the people were watching her!

Yo momma is so fat...when Jabba's guard from Star Wars pushed her down into the Sarlacc pit, the pit choked to death!

# YO MOMMA IS SO FAT...

Yo momma is so fat...when she did a bungee jump, she ended up all the way in Hell!

Yo momma is so fat...I feel like insulting her, but I'm from India, and cows are sacred in my country!

Yo momma is so fat...when she steps out in a yellow raincoat, the people yell, "TAXI!"

Yo momma is so so fat...when she sat on a monster truck she made it a low-rider!

# YO MOMMA IS SO UGLY...

Yo momma is so ugly...one day she wanted to participate in an ugly contest, but they said, "Sorry, amateurs only."

Yo momma is so ugly...Waldo said she is the reason he is hiding!

Yo momma is so ugly...when she walked into Wal-Mart they turned off the security cameras!

Yo momma is so ugly...she's the reason why Sonic the Hedgehog runs like crazy!

# YO MOMMA IS SO UGLY...

Yo momma is so ugly...she made an onion cry.

Yo momma is so ugly...that if they would measure one's ugliness bricks, they would call her the Great Wall of China!

Yo momma is so ugly...when she took a bath the water jumped out!

Yo momma is so ugly...she scared the shit out of the toilet!

Yo momma is so ugly...she gives Freddy Krueger nightmare!

# YO MOMMA IS SO UGLY...

Yo momma is so ugly...her mama had to tie a steak around her neck to get the dog to lick her!

Yo momma is so ugly...when she brought a cow into Tesco, one of the employees said, "Get that cow out of here," and the cow replied, "My bad, it won't happen again!"

Yo momma is so ugly...when she went to the beautician, it took 10 hours - and that was only for a quote!

Yo momma is so ugly...when she put on her make-up, it jumped off!

# YO MOMMA IS SO UGLY...

Yo momma is so ugly...she didn't just get hit with the ugly stick. They used the whole tree on her!

Yo momma is so ugly...when she went into a haunted house she came out with a job application!

Yo momma is so ugly...your father brings her to work so he doesn't have to kiss her goodbye!

Yo momma is so ugly...Fix-It Felix said, "I can't fix it!"

# YO MOMMA IS SO STUPID...

Yo momma is so stupid...she brought a spoon to watch the Super Bowl!

Yo momma is so stupid...she once canceled a hockey game because there was ice on the field!

Yo momma is so stupid...she tried to ring Taco Bell!

Yo momma is so stupid...she was yelling through a letter box, we asked her what she was doing, she said leaving a voicemail!

# YO MOMMA IS SO STUPID...

Yo momma is so stupid...when you were born in the hospital and she saw your cord, she exclaimed, "Oh, great, he comes with a cable!"

Yo momma is so stupid...she got hit by a cup, ran to the police and said she got mugged!

Yo momma is so stupid...she challenged a Ford Focus to a staring contest!

Yo momma is so stupid...she bought tickets to go see X-Box perform live!

# YO MOMMA IS SO STUPID...

Yo momma is so stupid...when you asked a color television for your 16th birthday, she replied, "Which color would you like, sweetie?"

Yo momma is so stupid...she tried to eat a power mac because she thought it was better than a big mac!

Yo momma is so stupid...when I said, "Drinks are on the house," she got a ladder!

Yo momma is so stupid...she thought a quarter-back was a charity!

# YO MOMMA IS SO STUPID...

Yo momma is so stupid...and fat, she signed up for an email account because she heard it contained spam!

Yo momma is so stupid...when she uses Hotmail she wears oven mitts!

Yo momma is so stupid...she ordered a cheeseburger from McDonald's and said, "Hold the cheese!"

Yo momma is so stupid...she went to the dentist to get bluetooth!

# YO MOMMA IS SO OLD...

Yo momma is so old...when she closes her eyes to relive the past, her memories are in black and white!

Yo momma is so old...her first Christmas was the first Christmas!

Yo momma is so old...she knew the rapper 50 Cent when he was only 25 Cent.

Yo momma is so old...that the key on Benjamin Franklin's kite was to her house!

# YO MOMMA IS SO OLD...

Yo momma is so old...when she was in high school they didn't teach history yet!

Yo momma is so old...her Social Security number is 1!

Yo momma is so old...her Bible is signed by the author!

Yo momma is so old...when the clerk told her to act her own age, she fell down and died on the spot!

Yo momma is so old...when she farts, dust comes out!

# YO MOMMA IS SO OLD...

Yo momma is so old...Maria asked her to babysit Jesus!

Yo momma is so old...her right arm fell off when I put my hand on her back!

Yo momma is so old...she knew Mr. Clean when he had an Afro!

Yo momma is so old...her first car was a Model T-Rex!

Yo momma is so old...her birth certificate says "EXPIRED!"

# YO MOMMA IS SO OLD...

Yo momma is so old...she sat next to Abraham in preschool!

Yo momma is so old...creationists deny her existence!

Yo momma is so old...she forgot her lipstick on Noah's ark!

Yo momma is so old...seeing Jurassic Park in the cinema brought back memories!

Yo momma is so old...when I asked for her ID, she handed me a rock!

# YO MOMMA IS SO HAIRY...

Yo momma is so hairy...when she lifted her armpit, Guns 'n' Roses busted through the door and started to play "Welcome to the Jungle!"

Yo momma is so hairy...she cut her hair and lost 35 pounds!

Yo momma is so hairy...Jane Goodall set up a base camp in her bedroom!

Yo momma is so hairy...when Bigfoot saw her he stole her camera to take a snapshot of her!

# YO MOMMA IS SO HAIRY...

Yo momma is so hairy...when she went to the movie theater to see Star Wars, all the fans went berserk and said, "IT'S CHEWBACCA!"

Yo momma is so hairy...she uses a lawnmower to shave her legs!

Yo momma is so hairy...Wookie is the only language she speaks!

Yo momma is so hairy...when she went to the pet store they locked her up in a cage!

# YO MOMMA IS SO SHORT...

Yo momma is so short...you can see her feet on her driver's license!

Yo momma is so short...when she tried to smoke weed she couldn't get high!

Yo momma is so short...when she went to meet Santa he said, "Go back to work!"

Yo momma is so short...she does back flips in the space under the door!

# YO MOMMA IS SO SHORT...

Yo momma is so short...she can 69 with Yoda!

Yo momma is so short...she committed suicide of the curb!

Yo momma is so short...she can tie her shoes while standing up!

Yo momma is so short...when she sits on a dime, her feet don't touch the ground!

Yo momma is so short...she needs a ladder to pick up a dime!

# YO MOMMA IS SO BALD...

Yo momma is so bald...they had to replace Mr. Clean!

Yo momma is so bald headed...she uses a toothpick as a comb!

Yo momma is so bald...when she takes a shower she gets brainwashed!

Yo momma is so bald...when I rub her head, I can see the future!

Yo momma is so bald...I can see what's on her mind!

# YO MOMMA IS SO NASTY...

Yo momma is so nasty...when she went to take a shower the soap-on-a-rope hung itself!

Yo momma is so nasty...when she farts the smoke alarm goes off!

Yo momma is so nasty...her shadow leaves a grease trail!

Yo momma is so nasty...her farts are classified as biological weapon!

# YO MOMMA IS SO MUCH ELSE!

Yo momma has so much dandruff in her hair...when she shook her head left and right, the school principal called a snow day!

Yo momma is so big...when she got hit by a bus she asked, "Who threw a rock at me?"

Yo momma's teeth are so yellow...when she smiles, traffic slows down!

Yo momma is breath smelled so bad...when she walked by a clock it said, "Tic Tac!"

# YO MOMMA IS SO MUCH ELSE!

Yo momma and the sun have a lot in common: they're huge, round, and your eyes start to hurt looking at it!

Yo momma is so ghetto...she had to steal a pair of shoes just to throw them over the power line!

Yo momma is so cross-eyed...she went to a movie and thought it was a double feature!

Yo momma is breath is so bad...people look forward to her farts!

# YO MOMMA IS SO MUCH ELSE!

Yo momma is so dark...when I clicked on her profile pic, I thought my phone died.

Yo momma is so crusty...Pizza Hut hired her as a consultant!

Yo momma is so thin...when it rains, she can dodge the raindrops!

Yo momma is so lazy...she has a remote for the TV remote!

Yo momma is like the sun: stare at her too long and you'll go blind!